Apr 2016

```
D1250683
```

Robin Hood

Tammy Gagne

Mitchell Lane
PUBLISHERS
P.O. Box 196
Hockessin, DE 19707
www.mitchelllane.com

Mitchell Lane
PUBLISHERS

Printing   1   2   3   4   5   6   7   8

Audie Murphy
Buffalo Bill Cody
The Buffalo Soldiers
Eliot Ness

Francis Marion
Robin Hood
The Tuskegee Airmen
Wyatt Earp

Library of Congress Cataloging-in-Publication Data
Gagne, Tammy.
 Robin Hood / by Tammy Gagne.
     pages cm. — (Fact or fiction?)
 Includes bibliographical references and index.
 ISBN 978-1-61228-950-2 (library bound)
 1. Robin Hood (Legendary character)—Legends. 2. Folklore—England.
 3. Outlaws—England—Juvenile literature. I. Title.
 PR2129.G34 2016
 820.9'351—dc23
                                                              2015003184

eBook ISBN: 978-1-61228-951-9

                                                                                            PBP

CONTENTS

Words in **bold** throughout can be found in the Glossary.

A GLADE in SHERWOOD:

The man known as Robin Hood has become a legend throughout the world. But many people have no idea whether or not he ever actually existed.

CHAPTER 1

Hero of the People

Nestled in the heart of England is the small city of Nottingham. Today it is home to a variety of tourist attractions. The most famous is Sherwood Forest—the legendary home of Robin Hood. Nottingham's library includes more than 700 different books about this outlaw, who is best known for stealing from the rich and giving to the poor. And it's not just Nottingham. The adventures of Robin Hood have become the subject of countless movies, cartoons, and stories around the globe. Nearly everyone knows his name and exploits.

But was Robin Hood a real, living person? Is his story based on actual events? Or is it merely a legend?

Like many legends, the story of Robin Hood includes both facts and fiction. The story has been told and retold for centuries. Certainly, it has changed along the way. One might compare the tale to the telephone game. In this popular classroom exercise, a sentence is whispered from one person to another until it reaches the other side of the room. By the time the last whisper has been spoken, the sentence has usually changed at least a bit. One person may have heard a word incorrectly. Another might have replaced a word or two to make the statement more exciting or funny. This is likely the case with Robin Hood as well.

According to the Nottinghamshire County Council, "No-one knows for sure whether the legend of Robin Hood was based on a real historical character. It is a subject which is still hotly debated amongst **scholars**."[1] One of those scholars is David Baldwin. A retired university professor, Baldwin is the author of *Robin Hood: The English Outlaw Unmasked.*

Baldwin says, "The story of Robin Hood is a mystery which has captured people's imaginations."[2] The author has a theory of why no one has been able to prove that this man actually existed in history. "One reason why researchers have failed to find the historical Robin Hood is that many of them have been looking in the wrong time and for the wrong person,"[3] he insists.

As Baldwin explains, "Robin Hood" may actually have been a nickname. While researching his book, he learned that during the thirteenth century, criminals were often called Robin Hood, Robert Hood, Robin Hude, or Robert Hude. Baldwin points out that both forms of the first name contain the word *rob*, which means "to steal." He adds that the word *hood* is something that can be used to hide one's identity. He claims that whoever was "Robin Hood" may have never been known by that name in his own lifetime.

Baldwin continues, "There are probably several outlaws whose deeds have contributed to the modern-day stories of Robin Hood. But I believe

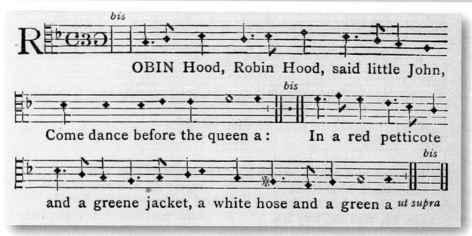

Many tales about Robin Hood came from ballads, or poems set to music, that were popular in centuries past.

there is one man whose career underpins the stories. His name is Roger Godberd and he was an outlaw who was active in the late 1260s."[4]

Early **ballads**, which are poems set to music as an easy way to remember them, tell the tale of Robin Hood. In them he stole deer from Sherwood Forest. He was captured by the Sheriff of Nottingham and imprisoned at Nottingham Castle. All of these things happened to Godberd as well. He even robbed churchmen like the fabled hero did.

Baldwin makes a convincing argument. But it is important to note that his theory is just one among many. Some people claim that Robin Hood lived during the reign of King Richard the Lionheart (1189–1199). Others place him in the time of King Edward II (1307–1327). With more than one hundred years separating the two periods, Robin Hood could have lived at any point within that span—if he even lived at all.

ROBIN HOOD

AND LITTLE JOHN

OR THE MERRY MEN OF SHERWOOD FOREST

BY PIERCE EGAN

Authors have written numerous books and stories about Robin Hood. The library in Nottingham alone contains more than 700 titles about the legendary outlaw.

CHAPTER 2

Not the Same Old Story

Each version of the Robin Hood story is just a little different from the others. In addition to the many books about the outlaw, numerous films have told his story. He has been played by Douglas Fairbanks (*Robin Hood*, 1922), Errol Flynn (*The Adventures of Robin Hood*, 1938), Sean Connery (*Robin and Marian*, 1976), Kevin Costner (*Robin Hood: Prince of Thieves*, 1991), and more recently, Russell Crowe (*Robin Hood*, 2010). In the animated 1973 Disney movie *Robin Hood*, the title character is depicted as a crafty fox. And the hero was even portrayed by Kermit the Frog on *The Muppet Show*.

What the stories have in common is a main character willing to stand up for the common people. Robin Hood does what no one else dares. He rebels against the sheriff and his men as they take land from Nottingham citizens—and tax them relentlessly on whatever isn't seized. In most stories the sheriff's plans are carried out through violence—sometimes even by way of murder.

Some stories show Robin's origins. *Robin Hood*, a children's book published in 2012 by David Calcutt, starts with a teenaged Robin. His skills with a bow

This woodcutting, a print made by carving into wood, depicts the setting of Nottingham in 1680.

and arrow far surpass those of the sheriff's men. *Robin Hood: His Life and Legend*, a 1979 book for young people written by Bernard Miles, also begins with Robin as a youngster. In this case, he is wrongly accused of poaching deer with the help of his dog.

The many variations of the tale make pinning down the truth nearly impossible. Most historians see the oldest stories as the best tool for separating fact from fiction. We know from the ballads noted by

David Baldwin that the early tales of Robin Hood mentioned his stealing deer. If those ballads are true, Miles's young Robin may not have been wrongly accused of **poaching** after all.

Among the earliest versions of Robin Hood's story is *The Gest of Robyn Hode*, a poem dating back to before 1510.[1] In this poem, Robin warns others to watch out for the Sheriff of Nottingham. It also speaks of Robin's unparalleled talent for archery, thereby supporting the stories that depict him as a supremely capable bowman.

Still other stories begin far from the city of Nottingham as Robin fights in the **Crusades**—an addition made to the story by Sir Walter Scott in his 1820 novel, *Ivanhoe*.[2] Before this time, though, Robin was described as a **yeoman**, a servant to a knight or a lord.

In *Ivanhoe* and most succeeding versions, the main character's proper name is Robin of Locksley. The son of a nobleman, he and his father are supporters of King Richard.

The nobleman Robin returns home from the Crusades to find that the Sheriff of Nottingham has murdered his father. He also learns that while King Richard and his men have been at war, the king's brother John has taken over the English throne. The real King John did indeed usurp the throne from his brother. But this fact alone does not prove that Robin Hood's story actually happened. Many stories are simply set in well-known periods of history. They fall under the category of historical fiction. Is Robin Hood one of them?

In the 2010 movie *Robin Hood* starring Russell Crowe, the main character isn't even the true Locksley heir. Instead, he is Robin Longstride, a soldier who is with Robert of Locksley when he dies in the Crusades. Before taking his last breath, Robert asks Longstride to return his sword to his father, Walter. Upon fulfilling the request, Longstride is asked to pose as Walter's son in an effort to protect his land from being taken by the greedy brother of the king. Again, the backdrop of this tale includes historical facts. But the story of Robin Longstride isn't among them.

To some movie critics, the introduction of Robin Longstride isn't the only problem with the film. In her review, Alex von Tunzelmann states, "Following in the footsteps of *Robin Hood: Prince of Thieves* and *Robin of Sherwood*, it mixes up the legend with the Crusades. It even goes further, and makes Robin responsible for the Magna Carta,"[3] an actual and important document that limited the power of the king. "Historically, this is riddled with impossibilities,"[4] she adds.

Whether he was a lord or something else, however, seems unimportant in the long run. Most stories depict Robin as unimpressed by status. In *Robin Hood: Prince of Thieves*, Robin states, "I've seen knights in armor panic at the first hint of battle. And I've seen the lowliest, unarmed **squire** pull a spear from his own body, to defend a dying horse. Nobility is not a birthright. It's defined by one's actions."[5] While these words were the work of

Hollywood screenwriters, they fit the image created by many stories of the legendary figure.

Some people argue that Robin Hood is more an idea than a person. They see him as a symbol of standing up for what is right, even in the face of great danger. This symbol is not unique to England. As newspaper columnist Margaret Wente writes, "Many cultures have Robin Hood figures. Japan has Nezumi Kozō, a successful burglar of samurai estates who was exiled and eventually beheaded. The Ukrainian Robin Hood is Ustym Karmaliuk, a serf who organized a series of rebel uprisings to attack rich landowners, and distributed the loot to the poor. He was captured many times, but always escaped, and was, as legend goes, impervious to bullets. There are Estonian, Hungarian, and Indian Robin Hoods. But nowhere is Robin Hood more celebrated than in the West, where he has endured through popular culture ever since medieval times."[6]

HERE LIES BURIED

LITTLE JOHN
THE FRIEND & LIEUTENANT OF
ROBIN HOOD
HE DIED IN A COTTAGE (NOW DESTROYE
TO THE EAST OF THE CHURCHYARD
THE GRAVE IS MARKED BY
THIS OLD HEADSTONE & FOOTSTONE
AND IS UNDERNEATH THIS OLD YEW TRE

Legend states that Little John dug his own grave in the Hathersage churchyard in Derbyshire, England. Caretakers added a stone marker to the site in 1935.

CHAPTER 3

Robin's Merry Men

Without a doubt Robin Hood is the best-known character within his tales. In addition, several other characters have emerged as major players over time. Some appeared in the earliest versions of the story and assumed larger roles in succeeding centuries. These characters are part of what have become known as Robin's Merry Men. This group of forest dwellers joins Robin in rebelling against the Sheriff of Nottingham.

One of these important characters is Little John. His name is a joke, as John is a huge man. According to a sixteenth-century ballad, he is seven feet tall, though that is likely to be an exaggeration. The official Nottinghamshire website states, "Little John was Robin's best friend right from the start. He appears in all of the six original tales and serves as a steadying influence on Robin's wild character. John has to have a lot of patience as Robin is moody, irritable and argumentative with him. They often fall out. Robin's temper gets him into all sorts of trouble so John is constantly coming to the rescue."[1]

In many versions of the story, Robin meets Little John while trying to cross a narrow bridge that spans a brook. Neither man will make way for the other. John challenges Robin to a duel with **quarterstaves**. The two men batter each other until John knocks Robin off the bridge into the water. Robin summons his followers, who threaten Little John. Robin tells his men to leave him alone because it was a fair fight. According to a ballad, Little John replies,

"'O here is my hand,' the stranger reply'd,
'I'll serve you with all my whole heart.'"[2]

Another well-known member of the outlaw group is Will Scarlet. According to the Nottinghamshire website, "Will appears in a supporting role in a number of the original tales."[3]

Will usually stands out for wearing the color red. Robin and the rest of his Merry Men are known for wearing bright green woolen clothing. The color is called Lincoln green after the English city where the cloth was first made. Interestingly, Will's clothing is almost certainly linked to his last name. But it wasn't always Scarlett. Earlier versions of the tale include several different last names for his character— including Scadlock, Scalok, Scarlock, and Scathelok.

In *Robin Hood: Prince of Thieves*, Will makes a surprising announcement—he is the outlaw's long-lost brother. This announcement is based on several earlier versions of the story, in which Will is a nephew or cousin of Robin.

A third character whom writers seem to love developing more and more is Friar Tuck. A clergyman who might have been the basis for Friar Tuck can be traced back to an early ballad, *Robin Hood and the*

Curtal Friar. In 1560, the play *Robin Hood and the Friar* names him Friar Tuck.[4] Centuries ago, the word curtal meant "wearing a short, or curtailed gown, easy to walk in." This was also the meaning of the word tuck.

Friar Tuck is almost always portrayed as a friendly but flawed clergyman. His character enjoys indulging in many things that preachers condemn. The most frequently mentioned of these is consuming mead, an alcoholic drink made from honey. Even children's books depict a

Like Robin Hood himself, Friar Tuck became a character in Sir Walter Scott's novel Ivanhoe.

less-than-**righteous** Friar Tuck. David Calcutt writes, "It's said that Friar Tuck in the Robin Hood stories was based on a real-life bandit friar who lived in Lincolnshire in the 1300s."[5]

The Nottinghamshire website also notes that a fifteenth-century chaplain was the leader of a gang of thieves. This real-life chaplain, named Robert Stafford, used the **alias** Friar Tuck.[6] In light of this historic detail, we can be almost sure that at least one Friar Tuck actually existed.

Some well-known actors have portrayed Robin Hood over the last century. Here, Douglas Fairbanks is seen in the role along with Enid Bennett as Maid Marian in 1922.

CHAPTER 4

A Lord in Need of a Lady

Over time, the character of Robin also developed into a romantic hero. This change to the story began with the addition of Maid Marian, who did not appear in the earliest versions of stories about the outlaw.

She was introduced as early as 1509.[1] At this time, though, she was very different from the Marian depicted in later versions of the Robin Hood tale. She also played far less of a role in the story than the character usually does today. Marian's name is thought to have come from a series of French songs about a medieval shepherdess. The stories were likely merged because the shepherdess Marian was in love with a young man named Robin.

By 1598, however, playwright Anthony Munday had transformed Marian into a young woman of noble birth in two plays about Robin Hood.[2] Stephen Knight asserts, "Whatever her origin, the first time a role of **substance** for a lady emerges in the outlaw myth is when its hero has become a lord, and so needs a lady."[3]

In *Robin Hood: Prince of Thieves*, Marian's character speaks a line that is a fitting match to Knight's thoughts about her character. When Robin

Hood tells Marian that he hopes to fall in love and settle down, she states, "Men speak conveniently of love when it serves their purpose."[4] This phrase is especially interesting in that her entire character as Robin's love interest may have been created to serve Munday's purpose.

A closer look at Munday's work suggests that Marian may have been a real person. A 1594 poem, *Matilda the Faire and Chaste Daughter of Lord R. Fitzwater* by Michael Drayton, tells the tale of a beautiful young woman who is pursued by King John. Because the piece reads much like Munday's play, it may seem like the poem is evidence that Maid Marian actually existed in history. But the fact is that the woman from Drayton's work had no relation to Robin Hood that Munday didn't invent.[5]

Even though it is unlikely that she was a real person, Marian has become an increasingly important character over the last century. Marian did not simply progress in status as time passed. She also grew in depth. Today many people see her as a **feminist**. Writer Adam Thorpe points out that ever since the 1922 film *Robin Hood*, Marian has been "as happy to take the **initiative** and wield a sword as any man."[6]

In *Robin Hood: Prince of Thieves*, Marian is first seen dressed in black with a metal fighting mask. Her character handles a sword as capably as a male. But even this modern version of the tale puts her in the role of damsel in distress before its end. When Robin comes to rescue her, Marian cries, "You came for me!"[7] He responds by telling her that he would die for her.

Some incredible art has been created as a result of the Robin Hood legend. This engraving depicting the marriage of Robin and Marion is found on the wall at Nottingham Castle.

In the 2010 *Robin Hood* movie, however, Marian is among those willing to risk their lives. Just before the battle scene on the beach, she shows up on horseback in full armor, ready to fight alongside Robin and his men. In terms of history, of course, this part of the story never happened. But millions of people watched the film—many of them young women—and saw a brave and powerful role model in Marian's character. And the strength of that character could be seen as very real indeed.

21

Since no one knows for certain whether Robin Hood ever existed, it is impossible to say what he may have looked like. Still, many artists have guessed at his appearance in their works.

CHAPTER 5

Many Theories, Few Facts

It is doubtful that historians will ever be able to prove or disprove Robin Hood's existence. Yet they will keep trying. Most historians agree with David Baldwin's opinion that if the outlaw was real, his name probably wasn't Robin Hood.

Roger Godberd is just one of the many people in history whom scholars claim are the real Robin Hood. An article in the *Nottingham Evening Post* states, "Several historical figures have been identified as potential origins for Robin Hood. The most likely is Robert Hod, later known as Hobbehod, who was a **tenant** of the Archbishop of York in Tudor times. He was called before York Assizes in 1225 and 1226 but fled, and is described in legal records as an outlaw."[1]

Writer Tony Rennell insists that if the outlaw we know as Robin Hood existed, he might not have even come from Nottingham. "According to 'A Geste of Robyne Hood and his Meiny'—an eight-part ballad in 456 verses, which was the first substantial account of him to appear in printed form—he haunted Barnsdale Forest in South Yorkshire."[2]

The writer suggests that long-ago fans of the poem may have read too much into a tiny part of it. The ballad states, "He did [poor] men much good."[3] It is possible that the entire concept of Robin Hood's stealing from the rich and giving to the poor came from this single line. This would have been a huge leap indeed.

Rennell also thinks Baldwin is wrong about Roger Godberd. He says, "There is a major difficulty in pinning the feathered cap on him as the real Hood, for Godberd was up to no good more than fifty years after the reigns of King Richard and King John when most of the Robin Hood tales . . . are set."[4] If Godberd is eliminated, many other men still might have been the real Robin.

According to Rennell, "Another possibility was the splendidly-named Fulk FitzWarin, who became an outlaw in the Welsh borders in the early thirteenth century after refusing to accept King John's verdict on a long-standing inheritance dispute. He was later one of the barons who forced John to sign the Magna Carta."[5] Perhaps Robin Hood did have a hand in making the document after all.

Yet another man who might have been the real Robin Hood was a monk named Eustace. Said to have taken arms against King John and fleeing into the forest, Eustace was known for wearing disguises. "He would hold up travelers and demand to know how much money they were carrying. Then he searched them and if they were telling the truth they kept it all. Liars lost the lot—a jolly ploy also attributed to Hood,"[6] says Rennell.

It is possible, even likely, that many real men played a small part in the creation of Robin Hood. Some were writers, others outlaws. According to the Nottingham County Council website, "The phrase 'Robinhood' became a nickname used in court records for an outlaw, and there is evidence of at least eight people before 1300 who adopted it or were given it as a **pseudonym**. The word 'hood' still means a gangster or outlaw in America. Probably, the real identity of Robin Hood will remain as elusive as the legendary outlaw. But one thing is sure: His popularity is as great now as it ever was, and forever linked in our imagination to ancient Sherwood Forest."[7]

People will continue to debate Robin Hood's existence. As Stephen Knight wrote, "I like to say, 'Of course he exists, we're talking about him.'" Knight's response may be funny. But it also makes an interesting point. As he stated, "There's a real myth which is living and breathing."[8]

Even legends have gravesites. Robin Hood's is said to be located at Kirklees Hall in West Yorkshire. This is also the location where many people believe the real Robin Hood died, but no one truly knows for sure.

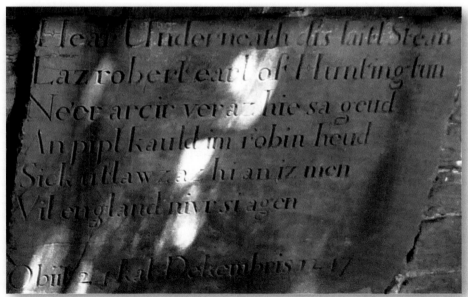

FACT OR FICTION?

Separating the facts from the fiction about Robin Hood is a difficult task. One might even call it an impossible one. The immense number of works that have been created about this legendary figure offer us plenty of information to consider. From ballads and books to films and even cartoons, it seems that Robin Hood's story has been told in every imaginable way. But the large number of different tales also makes the job of identifying the truth much more involved. We can, however, form some educated guesses based on historical evidence.

FICTION: The famous outlaw was named Robin Hood.

FACT: If a real "Robin Hood" actually existed, this likely wasn't his true name. He may have been nicknamed Robin Hood, after the act of "robbing" people or because thieves during this era often wore hoods to hide their identities.

FICTION: Robin Hood stole from the rich and gave what he took from them to the poor.

FACT: A ballad titled *A Geste of Robyne Hood and his Meiny* includes the line: "He did [poor] men much good." The idea that Robin Hood stole for the purpose of helping those less fortunate could have come from this one line of the poem.

FICTION: Known more formally as Robin of Locksley, Robin Hood was the son of a nobleman.

FACT: Stories of Robin Hood had been told for centuries when the first mention of "Robin of Locksley" appeared in Sir Walter Scott's novel 1820 novel, *Ivanhoe*. This detail stuck, as it has been included in most versions of the story from this point forward. But almost certainly it is not accurate.

FICTION: Will Scarlet is Robin's long-lost brother.

FACT: Early versions of Robin Hood's story describe Will as Robin's cousin or nephew, but not his brother. Not only was Will not Robin Hood's brother, he wasn't even Will Scarlet. The colorful surname likely came about because his last name sounded like the word scarlet. Earlier tales note Will's last name as Scadlock, Scalok, Scarlock, and Scathelok.

FICTION: Robin Hood's lady love was Maid Marian.

FACT: Perhaps the biggest piece of fiction about Robin Hood is his involvement with a young woman named Marian. No evidence of Marian's existence has been found. She does not even appear in the earliest versions of the story. This lady was likely added to the tale around the time that Scott turned Robin into a lord.

Chapter 1: Hero of the People
1. "Who was Robin Hood?" Nottinghamshire County Council. http://www.nottinghamshire.gov.uk/enjoying/countryside/countryparks/sherwood/sherwoodforesthistory/robinhoodhistory/
2. Chris Parsons, "Is this the grave of Robin Hood?" *Daily Mail*, April 2, 2011. http://www.dailymail.co.uk/news/article-1372334/Has-mystery-Robin-Hoods-identity-finally-solved-Historians-claim-farmer-led-band-highwaymen.html
3. David Baldwin, *Robin Hood: The English Outlaw Unmasked* (Stroud, Gloucestershire, England: Amberley, 2011), p. 9.
4. Stephen Moss, "In search of the real Robin Hood." *The Guardian*, May 11, 2010. http://mg.co.za/article/2010-05-11-in-search-of-the-real-robin-hood

Chapter 2: Not the Same Old Story
1. Stephen Knight, *Robin Hood: A Mythic Biography* (Ithaca, NY: Cornell University Press, 2003), p. 14.
2. Stephen Moss, "In search of the real Robin Hood." *The Guardian*, May 11, 2010. http://mg.co.za/article/2010-05-11-in-search-of-the-real-robin-hood
3. Alex von Tunzelmann, "Reel history special: Ridley Scott's Robin Hood—wide of the mark?" *The Guardian*, September 23, 2010. http://www.theguardian.com/film/2010/sep/23/ridley-scott-robin-hood-russell-crowe
4. Ibid.
5. *Robin Hood: Prince of Thieves* (film). Warner Brothers, 1991.
6. Margaret Wentes, "The true meaning of Robin Hood." *The Globe and Mail*, May 21, 2010. http://www.theglobeandmail.com/globe-debate/the-true-meaning-of-robin-hood/article4320091/

Chapter 3: Robin's Merry Men
1. Experience Nottinghamshire, The official tourism website of Nottinghamshire, Robin Hood's Merry Men. http://www.experiencenottinghamshire.com/robin-hood/robin-hood-legend/the-merry-men
2. Ibid.
3. Ibid.
4. Ibid.
5. David Calcutt, *Robin Hood* (Cambridge, MA: Barefoot Books, 2012), p. 108.
6. Experience Nottinghamshire.

Chapter 4: A Lord in Need of a Lady

1. Stephen Knight, *Robin Hood: A Mythic Biography* (Ithaca, NY: Cornell University Press, 2003), p. 59.
2. Experience Nottinghamshire, The official tourism website of Nottinghamshire, Robin Hood's Merry Men. http://www.experiencenottinghamshire.com/robin-hood/robin-hood-legend/the-merry-men
3. Knight, *Robin Hood*, p. 59.
4. *Robin Hood: Prince of Thieves* (film). Warner Brothers, 1991.
5. Knight, *Robin Hood*, p. 59.
6. Adam Thorpe, "Men in green: Bandit or hero?" *The Guardian*, April 30, 2010. http://www.theguardian.com/culture/2010/may/01/robin-hood-ridley-scott-outlaw
7. *Robin Hood: Prince of Thieves* (film).

Chapter 5: Many Theories, Few Facts

1. Dan Russell and Charlotte Abell, "Ten golden oldies that make our county great." Nottingham Evening Post, January 2, 2014.
2. Tony Rennell, "What has Hollywood done to Robin Hood?" Daily Mail, May 13, 2010. http://www.dailymail.co.uk/tvshowbiz/article-1277956/Tony-Rennell-What-Hollywood-Robin-Hood.html
3. Ibid.
4. Ibid.
5. Ibid.
6. Ibid.
7. Nottinghamshire County Council, *Robin Hood*. http://www.nottinghamshire.gov.uk/enjoying/countryside/countryparks/sherwood/sherwoodforesthistory/robinhoodhistory/
8. Stephen Moss, "In search of the real Robin Hood." *The Mail & Guardian*, May 11, 2010. http://mg.co.za/article/2010-05-11-in-search-of-the-real-robin-hood

GLOSSARY

alias (A-lee-uss)—an assumed or additional name

Crusades (croo-SADES)—series of Christian military expeditions in the eleventh, twelfth, and thirteenth intended to free the Holy Lands from Muslim control.

ballad (BAAL-uhd)—a poem telling a story of adventure, romance, or a hero suitable for singing; usually has stanzas of four lines with a rhyme on the second and fourth lines

feminism (FEM-uh-niz-uhm)—the theory supporting the political, economic, and social equality of the sexes

initiative (ih-NISH-uh-tiv)—a first step or movement

poach (POACH)—to hunt or fish unlawfully

pseudonym (SOO-doh-nim)—a fictitious name

quarterstaves (KWAWR-ter-staves)—strong hardwood poles between six and eight feet long, used long ago as weapons

righteous (RIE-chuss)—acting correctly

scholar (SKOL-uhr)—a person who has done advanced study in a special area

squire (SKWYR)—one who carries the shield or armor of a knight

substance (SUHB-stuhnss)—the subject matter of thought, discourse, study, etc.

tenant (TEN-uhnt)—one who occupies property owned by another person and pays rent to the owner

yeoman (YOH-muhn)—a servant in a royal or noble household

WORKS CONSULTED

Baldwin, David. *Robin Hood: The English Outlaw Unmasked*. Stroud, Gloucestershire, England: Amberley, 2011.

Knight, Stephen. *Robin Hood: A Mythic Biography*. Ithaca, NY: Cornell University Press, 2003.

Experience Nottinghamshire, The official tourism website of Nottinghamshire, Robin Hood's Merry Men. http://www.experiencenottinghamshire.com/robin-hood/robin-hood-legend/the-merry-men

The History Channel, *The Real Robin Hood*. http://www.history.com/topics/british-history/robin-hood

Knight, Stephen. *Robin Hood: A Mythic Biography*. Ithaca, NY: Cornell University Press, 2003.

The Official Website of the British Monarchy, Richard I Coeur de Lion ('The Lionheart') (r.1189–1199). https://www.royal.gov.uk/HistoryoftheMonarchy/KingsandQueensofEngland/TheAngevins/RichardICoeurdeLion.aspx

Moss, Stephen. "In search of the real Robin Hood." *The Mail & Guardian*, May 11, 2010. http://mg.co.za/article/2010-05-11-in-search-of-the-real-robin-hood

Moss, Stephen. "On the trail of the real Robin Hood." *Sydney Morning Herald*, May 1, 2010. http://www.smh.com.au/entertainment/movies/on-the-trail-of-the-real-robin-hood-20100430-tydj.html

Nottinghamshire County Council, Robin Hood. http://www.nottinghamshire.gov.uk/enjoying/countryside/countryparks/sherwood/sherwoodforesthistory/robinhoodhistory/

Parsons, Chris. "Is this the grave of Robin Hood? Historian claims farmer buried in an unmarked tomb is the outlaw behind the legend." *Daily Mail*, April 2, 2011. http://www.dailymail.co.uk/news/article-1372334/Has-mystery-Robin-Hoods-identity-finally-solved-Historians-claim-farmer-led-band-highwaymen.html

Rennell, Tony. "What has Hollywood done to Robin Hood?" *Daily Mail,* May 13, 2010. http://www.dailymail.co.uk/tvshowbiz/article-1277956/Tony-Rennell-What-Hollywood-Robin-Hood.html

Robin Hood (film), Universal Pictures, 2010.

Robin Hood: Prince of Thieves (film). Warner Brothers, 1991.

"Robin Hood's Merry Men," Experience Nottinghamshire now: The official tourism website of Nottinghamshire. http://www.experiencenottinghamshire.com/robin-hood/robin-hood-legend/the-merry-men

Russell, Dan and Charlotte Abell. "Ten golden oldies that make our county great." *Nottingham Evening Post,* January 2, 2014.

Thorpe, Adam. "Men in green: Bandit or hero?" *The Guardian*, May 1, 2010. http://www.theguardian.com/culture/2010/may/01/robin-hood-ridley-scott-outlaw

von Tunzelmann, Alex. "Reel history special: Ridley Scott's Robin Hood—wide of the mark?" *The Guardian*, September 23, 2010. http://www.theguardian.com/film/2010/sep/23/ridley-scott-robin-hood-russell-crowe

Wentes, Margaret. "The true meaning of Robin Hood." *The Globe and Mail*, May 21, 2010. http://www.theglobeandmail.com/globe-debate/the-true-meaning-of-robin-hood/article4320091/

World Wide Robin Hood Society, http://www.robinhood.ltd.uk/

FURTHER READING

Bradbury, Jim. *Robin Hood: The Real Story of the English Outlaw*. Stroud, Gloucestershire (England): Amberley Publishing, 2013.

Calcutt, David. *Robin Hood*. Cambridge, MA: Barefoot Books, 2012.

Cody, Matthew. *Will in Scarlett*. New York: Knopf Books for Young Readers, 2013.

Rennsion, Nick. *Robin Hood: Myth, History & Culture*. Harpenden, UK: Oldcastle Books, 2012.

ON THE INTERNET

History Channel, Robin Hood
http://www.history.com/topics/british-history/robin-hood

Experience Nottinghamshire
http://www.experiencenottinghamshire.com/robin-hood

World Wide Robin Hood Society
http://www.robinhood.ltd.uk/

INDEX

ABOUT THE AUTHOR

Tammy Gagne is the author of numerous books for adults and children, including *Eliot Ness* and *Tuskegee Airmen* for Mitchell Lane Publishers. She resides in northern New England with her husband and son. One of her favorite pastimes is visiting schools to speak to kids about the writing process.